AF560106

Contractual Labour in Agricultural Sector

Contractual Labour in Agricultural Sector

By
Dr. S.N. Tripathy
Deptt. of Economics
Aska Science College
Aska (Orissa)

First Published - 2000

Reprinted - 2025

ISBN: 978-81-7141-534-2

Contractual Labour in Agricultural Sector

Published by:

DISCOVERY PUBLISHING HOUSE
4383/4B, Ansari Road, Darya Ganj
New Delhi-110 002 (India)
Phone: +91-11-23279245, 23253475; 43596065
E-mail: discoverybooksindia@gmail.com
orderdphbooks@gmail.com
web: www.discoverypublishinggroup.com

Printed at:
Infinity Imaging Systems
Delhi

Dedicated to my father

Sri Sisirakanta Tripathy

Preface

In Pre-nineteenth century in India, the agrarian society consisted of largely self-sufficient village communities. In such village communities, the cultivators and artisans had lived together for centuries. They had their traditional method of exchanging the agricultural product and services mutually beneficially to each other. The cultivation process was carried on with the help of his own family members in an agricultural household. Agriculture and handicrafts were integrated and inter-dependent. The landless agricultural labourers earned their livelihood by selling their labour and earning wages. The census reports indicated that there were less than 20 per cent of agricultural population in the pre-nineteenth century.

But it was due to land settlement introduced by the British in India, the Zamindars were declared not as the agents of revenue collection but as the full proprietors of the areas over which their rights of land revenue collection extended.

Thus, by the force and authority of the British India, millions of cultivators were transformed from peasant proprietorship into tenants-at-will. "In the entire history of mankind, ancient and modern, one would look in vain for a parallel to this classic example where in so many were sacrificed in such a short period so that a few may prosper and rule". The effect of such a policy was advantageious as it supported the pillars of British rule in India.

In addition to the heavy and rigid revenue demands of the British Government, uncertainty of crops due to droughts and famines have detrimental effects on farming community. Thus, there were twenty-two officially declared famines and unaccountable non-official famines by the end of 19th century in the British India. Naturally, these resulted in impoverishment and poverty of the agricultural labourers in India, who ultimately were forced to borrow for their survival needs. The Famine Commission of 1901 had remarked, ".....the cultivators held their lands, helped to bring this result about. The rigidity of the revenue system forced them into debt, while the valuable property which they held made it easier to borrow. It was in this process that on the one hand lands of un-protected cultivators began to be concentrated into the hands of a few money lenders, on the other hand, large masses of peasantry began to roll down the social ladder as tenant-at-will and landless labourers. It was in this process of disposession of the peasantry that the large and distant class of landless labourers was born."

Thus, it was the callousness of the British Government's policy towards the agrarian population of India, which held the latter in the grip of poverty and misery. On the other hand, the Indian Peasants have a long and unrecorded history of sporadic bloody struggle against such inhuman policies.

We can outline the types of agricultural labourers as manifested in the pre-independence British India.

The lowest position in the socio-economic ladder was occupied by the bonded or semi-free labourers. This class of labourers have been recognised as 'agrarian serfs'.

It has been generally believed that the important cause of accepting the position of bond slave or bonded labour by the agricultural labourers was the urgent need of labourers to secure advance of money from the moneylenders and landlords. This through the social customs, traditions and rural power structure had their role but monetary factor pre-dominated all other considerations for bondage. The advance of money, for social functions and needs or any other purpose, was more in the nature of mutual recognition that the system of bondage was sanctioned by both parties of debtor and creditor. The debtor-creditor relationship was turned into master and slave relation and thus, bonded labour was the consequent result.

Because of unemployment and underemployment serfdom or bondage was accepted as a source of income and livelihood in most part of the country during the 19th and early part of the 20th Century. The system of bonded labour during the British India was more in the southern India mainly in the Madras presidency in the states of Andhra Pradesh, Orissa, etc.

The Royal Commission on Agriculture remarked that "in many cases, the tiller of land is subject to conditions which make his status approach much more closely to that of a labourer than an independent cultivator." Thus, we behold a very large proportion of labourers in India belonged to the category of tenants-at-will and share-croppers.

The landless labourers formed the third category of agricultural labourers in India. These labourers form an amorphous mass of a floating reserve migrating from place to place in search of employment. The employment may be on the agricultural land during peak seasons or in industries or any kind of manual jobs. The Royal Commission on Agriculture has aptly remarked that seventy-five per cent of the labour employed in 15 large Sugar Mills in Bihar and Orissa composed of such migratory labourers. (Royal Commission on Agriculture, Report pp. 576–77).

The last category of labourers as noted in the Report on labour conditions in India (London, 1928, p. 36) was wage labourers. The said Report pointed out that "in Assam tea, the Sweat, hunger and despair of a million Indians enter year by year."

In our country most of the people in the poor strata of society eke out a living only through the sell of their labour. It is, therefore, of paramount significance on the part of labouring class to visualise the changes taking place in the labour market. As we know, changes in the labour market are influenced by agriculture through its casual links with the labour market. An increasing trend in agricultural supply curve results in rising labour demand curve leading to expansion of employment and wage rate. Growth of agriculture has its impact of accelerating employment in other sectors through the demand linkages. On the supply side, factors like reosurce base, socio-economic background considerably influence the behaviour of the households to supply labour. On the contrary, we witness the barriers of castes, religion, language, obstructing the mobility of labour. The risk of unemployment is to a greater extent due to uncertainty in the labour market. Thus, the wage rate as well as wage labour are exposed to fluctuations.

Thus, agricultural labour households consisting of marginal and small operational holdings constitute the sizeable section of the rural poor. The incidence of poverty is manifested among this sections of the rural population. Obviously, the factors like the access to land and other inputs, the capabilities of these people to increase productivity and finally, the level of income of the agricultural households determine the extent of poverty among this category of households.

Economists furnish opinions to reduce poverty by various techniques. One such opinion is through sustained growth rate of agricultural production. This, in turn, should be on the basis of adoption of cost-reducing technology. Further, this should be accompanied by sustained expansion of employment in the non-agricultural sector and informal sector.

But ironically, we witness that the modern technology and subsequent commercialisation of agriculture leads to polarize the peasantry into large commercial farms and wage labourers. Thus, the ultimate result has been he limited access to land by the poverty-stricken peasants and shift in their occupational structure. The shift has been found from self-employed cultivator to the wage labourer.

The rapid growth of population further aggravates the problem through high land-man ratio or heavy pressure on land and sub-division of land holding leading to increase in the number of marginal and small farmers. Thus, this demographic change leads to occupational change of rural population from marginal farmers to wage labour.

The key to solves the problem of rural poverty is through poverty eradication programmes which may bring about employment generation, asset creation and increase in the standard of living of the agricultural labourers.

Unfortunately, all developmental efforts can not bring desired results so long as the rigidity in the rural socio-economic structure is not broken. The extent of inequality and skewed distribution of wealth and income has jeoparadise all our efforts to remove poverty. The factors like close nexus between the rural affluents and the political stalwarts, corruption deep rooted in the economy has created strong strumbling-blocks in the way to reducing in equality and conferring the fruits of planning and development at the grassroot level. Thus, educating the poor and downtrodden, creating consciousness among the agricultural labourers about their rights and duties, the labour-laws etc.; organising them for fighting against the social dogmas and evils are highly indispensable for bringing out the desired results in ameliorating the economic conditions of poor agricultural labourers. The task ahead is very herculean indeed. It needs the co-operation of

NGO's, Policy makers, educated people and the labourers themselves.

With a view to liberalising the economy and integrating it with the world economy, for reaching policy changes were introduced in India since 1991. The policy changes were introduced as a part of macro-economic stabilisation and structural adjustment policies (SAP) as suggested by the World Bank and International monetary fund (IMF). However, the adjustment policy did not make any reference to agriculture. But, the macro economic policies are having their impact an agricultural sector of the Indian economy. Because, the agricultural sector is the crucial sector in providing employment and income to the Indian population and has its diversified and multi-dimensional links with the growth of other sectors of the economy. Specifically, the new economic policies, have their strong and direct influence on agricultural output, prices, employment and technology, domestic price reforms which liberated agriculture from internal controls and rise prices of agricultural output are expected to have positive impact on agricultural growth.

The present study has been divided into four chapters.

Chapter 1 deals with the introduction and the framework of the study alongwith the relevant literature surveyed and the methodology adopted for the purpose of the study.

Chapter 2 is devoted exclusively to the history of agricultural labourers in India with special reference to Orissa.

In Chapter 3, we examine the socio-economic problems of contractual agricultural labourers with the help of primary data analysis.

Chapter 4, summarises the findings of the study alongwith a few suggestions.

Originally, this study was conducted because of the financial assistance provided by the University Grants Commission under Minor Research Project to College teachers for undertaking research in social work. I, therefore, express my deep gratitude to the authorities of the UGC for their consideration of the topical importance of this study as well as for providing fund for the same.

I must acknowledge the help and support extended by my wife Meera in arranging tables, charts and in checking the typed receipt with the Original report, I owe a special debt to my son Sameer and daughter Sunita who remained deprived of my love and affection during the period of this study.

I shall feel amply rewarded, if the work is of some help in comprehending the complex problems of agricultural households and in improving the organisational machinery to tackle them.

I express my heart-felt thanks to the agricultural labourers and attached agricultural labourers whose responses and interviewed. schedules have enriched the analysis of 'contractual labourers' socio-economic features.

However, I am solely responsible for the misconceptions and mistakes or improper analysis of observations, if any, made in this study.

S. N. Tripathy

Contents

1
Introduction

In this chapter an attempt has been made to portray the origin and growth of agricultural labour in Orissa with special reference to contractual labour. Brief out-line of the objectives of the study, the methodology adopted, scope of the study and the scheme of the study has also been made.

Under the capitalistic mode of production, labour power itself known as a commodity used in the production process for exchange. The level of employment as well as wages are determined simultaneously in the labour 'market' which reflects the aggregate results of supply and demand decisions of capitalistic producer. Labourers motive to supply labour is guided by leisure-income preferences and demand for labour by profit prospects of the producer. As capital and labour are considered as mobile factors for producers, all labour processes are inter-connected through the market.

In the context of Indian economy, labour processes and labour exchange systems have structurally different features. Depending upon the structure of economy, the labour exchange processes and production relations differ region-wise in various parts of country. As a result, we behold a spectrum of labour system prevailing in India.

An army of cultivators depending on small sub-divided holdings better termed as subsistence farmers have been classified as Cultivators in the census report but in reality they are Agricultural labour.

Landless labourers belonging to other category are without family enterprise mainly dependent upon wage-employment are alternatively know as casual labourers.

The National Sample Survey (NSS) rounds adopted 'Labour force' approach to consider variations in the level of employment over shorter intervals. The population is divided into three categories :

i The employed, reporting gainful activity over the (short) reference period such as 'one week'.

ii The unemployed, not so engaged but are actively seeking work (in later rounds amended to include those who may not be actively seeking work, but are available for work).

iii Persons not in the labour force.

Though on the plus side the NSS approach seems to caputre the seasonal element in rural employment through its methods of 'sub-rounds'. Also it includes the irregular or casual nature of employment by introducing shorter reference periods. However, the problem essentially remains. For example, construction women labourers who enter into hired labour market temporarily or occasionally to supplement their household income, maynot report themselves to be included in the labour force.

It is obvious from the discussion that problems are there in the computation of 'labour force participation rate' for females and in the aggregate. Again, the problem of work intensity is also found in the NSS approach.

In India, rural, labourers adopt time stretching activities due to low income and general lack of adequate work opportunity. Such activities like cattle grazing or picking the scattered ripped plants from the agricultural fields, cow-dung collections and other related works by the children of the agricultural labourers and even the rooting out the shrubs stones from the agricultural land by the female labourers in order to keep the land in better cultivable condition for ensuing year—are not included in NSS approach.

Keeping in view these conceptual problems that have been associated with secondary sources of data, we have decided to collect data from primary source by field study.

Agricultural Labour

Agricultural labourers constitute a large section of rural population in India. They work as wage earners, casual workers and are organised from socially and economically backward classes. There has been a sharp rise in the number and proportion of agricultural labourers in the rural work-force and of agricultural households. The percentage of agricultural households among all rural households for the country as whole increased from 22 per cent in 1964–65 to 31 per cent in 1983, 40 per cent during 1991.

The most distressing fact which has been reckoned with is the development of landless agricultural labourers consequent upon pauperisation and alienation on land of the poor peasantry. Because of feudalistic forms and practices still determining social relations in the rural sector with acute unemployment problem, in the absence of non-agricultural labourers becomes more complex. This is apprarently true when we find he attached labour households constituting 9.7 per cent of the total agricultural household in 1950–51, increased to 26.63 per cent by the end of sixties.

It has been observed that the gains of production and productivity in agricultural sector have been substantially monopolised by the landlords or land-owners.

The minimum wage fixed by the Government at the centre and state is of some use if the same is above the prevailing level fixed by customs or practices. But in reality, wages prescribed under minimum wages act are usually fixed below the prevailing wage rate. Secondly, there is no machinery or if at all exists, is ineffective for enforcement of such minimum wages.

The above analysis brings to light that the poor agricultural labourers are victims of cruel exploitation and deprivation under the present socio-economic, political frame.

Contractual Labour

That apart, as employment of agricultural labourers are mainly casual in nature, engaged either annually or seasonally by landlords depending upon the size of agricultural holding and operations. In the State of Orissa, there are regular farm servants : they are either mature male labourers known as Guti or Kuthia or Halia. The contract is informal, oral and personalised. Rural labourers who are attached to the landlords or big farmers on certain terms and conditions are known as attached labourers or contractual labourers. They are generally appointed or terminated on DOLAYATRA the day before *Holi* festival, as most of them are illiterate and unable to follow the

English calender. Such attached or contractual labourers which is widely found in rural villages of Orissa are appointed on certain conditions.

The fact that labour as an input is heterogeneous in character. They differ in their duration of contract, basis of payment, frequency of payment, mode of payment, nature of work, dependence/dominance, inter linkage with land or credit market etc.

In a village economy the terms and conditions of contracts in tenancy, wage labour and credit transactions are inter-related. Imperfections in the factor markets get reinforced by such inter-linkages.

The landlord-cum-employer may get underpaid labour services on his own farm by means of his power of wealth, political strength and dominance in the land-lease market. The creditor-landlord may influence his tenancy of his freedom in decision making. The landlord may also increase the rent by realising the interest on loans at the time of harvest sharing. Surveys conducted by Government organisations fail to capture the intricacies of these inter-relationships. Such general surveys do not focus on the linkages of land-ownership or land-lease pattern with wage labour or credit contracts. The rural enquiries by National Sample Survey Organisation, Reserve Bank of India, Village Survey carried out by Agro-Economic Research Centres in various parts of India do not focus on the inter-relationships of contracts.

In the light of the aforesaid analysis it is imperative to study the problems of contractual labour in agricultural sector of orissa.

Overview of Literature

A good deal of studies have been made in recent years with regard to the problems of agricultural labourers. Important studies relating to agricultural labourers in Indian states have been out-lined by many authors.

Sunghvi (1969)[1] examined the process of adoption of agrarian economy to the growth of surplus labour in agriculture in relation to its effect on total farm output, on the size and composition of the labour force on the span of the harvesting period, etc. The study throws light on the consequences of the growth of surplus manpower in agriculture and the utilisation of surplus labour in agriculture for economic development.

J.S. Uppal (1973)[2] has elaborated the relevance of different categories of disguised unemployment with reference to socio-economic conditions in rural sector of under-developed countries.

G. Partha Sarathy and G.D. Rama Rao (1974)[3] conducted a study in the state of Andhra Pradesh, pertaining to employment and unemployment of rural labour especially, landless labourers. The study suggests that government should increase the level of expenditure for employment programme, provide innovation and devotail the programme, provide innovation and devetail the programmes keeping in view the development needs of the agricultural labourers.

Prof. Aziz (1979)[4] in his study emphasised on organising agricultural labourers in India.

Seshadri (1983)[5] presents various facts and themes of rural unrest since independence.

Jain (1985)[6] studied the socio-economic conditions of women agricultural labourers in the state of Rajasthan. Some of the problems observed by him are paucity of land, social pressure, problems of work environment etc.

Mita Bhadra (1986)[7] examined the conditions of plantation women workers.

Rural labour Enquiry (1983)[8] presents the analysis of data relating to wages and earnings of agricultural households in India.

Dr. Harnek Singh (1986)[9] observed that most of the agricultural labourers are illiterate and belong to low castes in the rural areas. Green revolution has enhanced their wage and thereby, living standard.

Venkatnarayan (1987)[10] made a study in the Warangle District of Andhra Pradesh relating employement, wages and living conditions of agricultural labourers in Kuttand and Cannanore districts of Kerala State.

Prof. Nair (1987)[11] has made an attempt to study the employment, wage payment, income and consumption pattern and asset position of agricultural labourers in Kuttand and Cannanore districts of Kerala State.

Prof. V.R. Kolte (1989)[12] has made a study in the state of Maharashtra with regard to development of small and marginal farmers through government sponsored agricultural programmes.

Sarap (1989)[13] studied the trends in wage rates and living conditions of agricultural labourers in Orissa.

V.K. Ramachandran (1990)[14] in his research study has presented the picture of inequality among rural households inter-generational occupational change, employment position, seasonality of employment, wages and indebtedness of agricultural labourers.

Sarap (1992)[15] examined the various types of contractual arrangements in agricultural labour markets in western Orissa.

Thus, a plethora of works by various authors/researchers through light on various aspects of agricultural labourers in different states of India. However, studies on agricultural labourers in the state of Oirssa is extremely limited. So far no proper study on contractual agricultural labour in Ganjam District of Orissa has been conducted. Therefore, the present study attempts to fill the research gap and to highlight new literature on conditions of contractual labour in agricultural sector of Orissa.

Scope of the Study

The scope of the study is confined to two blocks, Digapahandi and Aska of Ganjam district of (Orissa). These two blocks have been selected due to the fact that these two blocks are the working places of the researcher for the last 18 years.

Objectives of the Study

The study has been designed with the following objectives :

i. The study aims at analysing the history of agricultural labourers in India with special reference to Orissa.

ii. The study examines the existing literature on agricultural labour and to trace out the research gap.

iii. To examines the types of contractual arrangement which prevail in Ganjam district (Orissa) in various types of agricultural operations and their linkages.

iv. Finally, to provide a policy thrust to ameliorate the condition of landless agricultural labourers.

Methodology

The present study, truly speaking, is first of its kind on Orissa, has been designed to present a socio-economic profile and living conditions of agricultural labourers, hired (Contractual) labour.

In this context, it is worthwhile to mention that available literature on agricultural labourers in Orissa is both limited and inadequate.

Census reports provide only the number of agricultural labourers, occupational distribution of workers etc. However, data relating to socio-economic condition of landless agricultural labourers are not available from such reports. In view of this absence of data, village studies are highly essential to catch a glimpse of truth liberally diluted in the socio-economic mileu of rural labour force.

Sampling Design

Data relating to family size, caste composition, mode and method of payment, hours of work, level of literacy, extent of indebtedness, socio-economic profile are collected through personal interview with the help of structured questionnaire.

In addition to the questionnaire method of collecting data, observation relevant to the study have been recorded in the form of field note.

Selection of the Field

Keeping in view the constraints of time and cost, it was decided to collect data for this enquiry from two blocks namely Aska and Digapahandi. Two villagers in each block and thus, 4 villagers of Ganjam district have been surveyed.

In addition to the primary source of data, secondary sources of data have been accumulated from Census report, Journals, books to supplement this study.

Data Processing

The collected field data have been processed and analysed in various tables followed by their findings/analysis. Simple percentage calculations have been made to draw some meaningful conclusions.

Period of the Study

The study has been conducted during Dec. '96 to April, '98 at different intervals, keeping in view the convenience of the contractual agricultural labourers.

As it has been mentioned earlier, in view of the financial implications in such field studies, and other busy schedules of the researcher and academic works, the researcher could not survey more villages.

However, all endeavours have been undertaken to make the study just, appropriate and genuine so as to generalize the findings for the district as well as the state. It is hoped, that the study will immensely benefit the planners, policy makers, and demographers, social-scientists, labour administrators and researchers to formulate policy measures.

Limitation of the Study

Undoubtedly, the study has some limitations which are out-lined below :

i) The information provided by the contractual labourers depend on their memory as they have no written record or available evidences to furnish.

ii) In certain cases, the presence of the land-lord during the period of interview has restricted the scope of true expression by the contract labourers, relations to some crucial issues.

Scheme of the Study

The study have been represented in the following four chapters:

Chapter 1 : Introduction

This chapter is devoted towards the discussion of over-view of literature, methodology and objectives of the study alongwith chapterization.

Chapter 2 : Agricultural Labour : A Historical Overview

The origin and history of agricultural labourers have been outlined in this chapter with special reference to Orissa state.

Chapter 3 : Socio-economic Problems of Contractual Agricultural Labourers

With the help of sample household study, this chapter examines the socio-economic features of contractual labourers in Orissa.

Chapter 4 : Concluding Observations and Policy Implication of the Study.

This chapter summarises the findings of the study alongwith policy implications.

Bibliography

References

1. Sanghvi, Prafulla : Surplus manpower in Agriculture and Economic development. Asia Publishing House, New Delhi, (1996).
2. Uppal, J.S. : Disguised unemployment in an under-developed economy : its nature and measurement, Asia Publishing House, New Delhi (1973).
3. G. Parthasarthy & G.D. Rama Rao : Employment and unemployment of rural labour and the crash problems (The study of west Godavari district) Andhra University Press, Waltair, 1974.
4. Aziz, Abdul : Organising Agricultural labour in India : A personal Minerva Associates, Calcutta, 1979.
5. K. Seshadri : Rural unrest in India. Intellectual Publishing House, New Delhi, 1983.
6. Jain, M. : Metholi Revisited : An Account of camp process of Agricultural Women Workers, Nov. 1985, National Labour Institute, Noida. (Unpublished).
7. Bhadra, Mita : Plantation women workers and their commitment to Industrial work, Man in India : Vol. 66(3), Sept. 1986, pp. 233–234.
8. Rural Labour Enquiry (1983) : Report on wages and Earnings of Rural labour Households, Labour Bureau, Shimla.
9. Singh, Harnek : Agricultural workers in Punjab : Their Role and commitment, Guru Nanak Dev University, (1986) Ph.D. Thesis (unpublished).
10. K. Venkatnarayan : Impact of Socio-economic factors on employment, wages and living conditions of selected villages in Warangal District, *Indian Dissertation,* 15(3) July–Sept., 1986, pp. 282–289.
11. N.K.A. Nair : Agricultural labour in Kerala : A Pilot Study, ICSSR Research, *Abstract quarterly,* Vol. –XVI No. 1 and 2, January–July, 1987, pp. 64–71.
12. Kotle, V.R. : Development of Small and Marginal Farmers (A case study of Vidarbha Region of Maharastra, Classical Publishing Company, New Delhi (1989).
13. Sarap, Kalish : Trends in wage rates and living conditions of Agricultural labourers in Orissa, Man and Development, Vol. 11 (3), Sept., 1989, pp. 113–123.

14. V. K. Ramachandran : Wage labour and Unfreedom in Agriculture : The Indian case study, Clanendon Press, Oxford, 1990.

15. Sarap, Kalish : "Changing contractual Arrangement in Agricultural labour market : Evidence from Orissa", *Economic and Political Weekly*, 26(52), p. 167–A176, 1992.

2
Agricultural Labour : A Historical Overview

An attempt has been made in this chapter to explore the genesis of the agricultural labourers in the state of Orissa by analysing the historical perspectives. The socio-economic scenario existing in the pre-independent era has been exhibited through the data collected from various reports and commissions. Besides, the factor like decay of village industries, growth of landless labourers, system of agency administration, the Mammol system and other exploitative labour system have been studied at length. Basically, the historical causes of backwardness of agrarian community in Orissa has been portrayed.

Pre-Independence Period

The advent of British rule in India and specifically in Orissa, brought a great transformation in the economic life of agricultural community. The Britishers were mainly a commercial group whose main interest was to exploit India in order to gratify their interests. This had apparently, adversely effected the agricultural and land revenue policy. The Britishers followed a policy which led to artificial enhancement of land value. Thus, speculation of land and escalation of prices were the sequel.

As a result, a new class of Parasites grew in Orissa which held under its control the available land. Thus, land became the monopoly of rich and the rest of the society became mere tenants.[1] This deplorable state of affair continued till the 19th century and crippled the agricultural community as a whole.[2]

Recurring Drought and Flood

The Britishers remarked that Orissa was beset with problems of natural calamities. Flood and famine, were the common natural horrors experienced in Orissa. In 1803, 1806, 1809, 1813, 1817, 1828, 1830, 1837 and 1842 Orissa had suffered due to severe droughts.[3]

Floods of severe magnitude were also experienced during 1815, In 1831 a great cyclone especially in Baleswar were found. In the Second part of 19th century, Orissa, suffered due to repeated floods in 1851, 1853, 1855, 1856, 1857, 1862, 1868, 1874, 1879, 1880, 1881, 1885, 1892, 1895, 1896 and 1900. In 1866, 1872, 1874 and 1892 there were cyclones which had affected the agro-economic condition seriously.[4]

The zamindars of Orissa were apathetic to the local people and cultivators. Most of them were from Bengal who had no sympathy for local Oriya people.

Export of rice from Orissa to Bengal in huge quantity were made. The report of the famine inquiry commission of 1867 bears the testimony to the fact that prior to 1866, the annual export of grain from Orissa was 20 thousand tonnes for last six years. In 1865, the export was to the extent of 35 thousand tonnes. Thus, it is obvious, the famine of 1866 was not due to natural causes but due to the callous attitude of the zamindars. To add to this problem; the Zamindars deliberately neglected cultivation with the hope of low assessment in land revenue.[5]

It is aptly remarked that lack of interest to improve the socio-economic conditions of Orissa, the unfavourable method of land revenue administration were responsible to keep more than six lakhs people of the province either in slavish or semi-slavish condition.[6]

In the early part of 20th century, it was found that the material condition of the peasants were miserable, inspite of investments made for their development.[7]

Various annual Administrative Reports of Orissa from 1866–67 to 1904–05 also corroborate to the above facts. These reports manifested that there prevailed extreme form of poverty and destitution among a considerable portion of agricultural population through out the period.

Accounting Factors for General Poverty

In Orissa, during 1858 to 1905, the population grew up by about 50%. It rose from 2319192 to 41511239 in 1901 during period review.[8] This high growth of population had server impact on land. Unfortunately, industries to provide employment were also developed.

Decay of Village Industries

The concentration of people on land was aggravated by the decay of village industries. Once upon a time, cloth making was the Principal industry. Even female members of the high class cultivators were engaged in making thread. But with the increase if foreign importation, it was forsaken and relegated to lower classes. According to the census returns of 1892, there were only 59,363 weavers in Cuttack, 56767 in Baleswar and about 19500 in Puri. The weavers were still famous for superior type of manufacturing. But cloth making in the province didn't pay in competition with imported goods from Manchester. Thus, the village industries died which had been supporting a large number of people. Those who were depending to eke-out a living, remained on the verge of starvation.[9,10]

As already pointed out, the export of food grains, apathy of the Zamindars, heavy pressure on land, decay of village industries all resulted in the great famine of 1866.

The scarcity of food grain and rise in the prices of food hard-heated the poor agricultural labourers in Orissa. Thus, the foregoing analysis brought to light that while the destruction of local industries compelled the masses to take agriculture as their main pursuit, unfavourable land revenue policy filled the cup of their misery.

The enhancement of rent, imposition of illegal cesses and absentee landlordism proved harmful to the agriculturist. Being ignorant they were not in a position to resist injustice and the government also did not take special measures protecting their interest.[11] Whatever little efforts were made to protect the agriculturists from the vagaries of monsoons, became inadequate to save the crops of the entire province. It had been reported that frequent crop failure on account of flood or drought plunged the roots in debt to Mahazans or Zamindars. They seldom managed to recover from them. Maddox remarked, "Thus whenever income is cut-short due to failure of crops or when the expenditure necessary from special occasions, which generally occur once or twice in every generations was to be bear, the ryot must fall in debt".[12] The aforesaid fact has been supplemented by R.C. Dutta, the Commissioner of Orissa. Dutta wrote in 1896, "Nevertheless, the majority of the cultivator are in debt, and always remain in debt to the Mahajans. They borrow paddy from the village Granaries, pay-off with high interest after the harvest and begin to borrow after they have consumed the surplus."

Wide-spread Poverty

Nagendranath Banerjee in agriculture Report on Cuttack, published in 1893, estimated that 75% of the agriculturists remained almost in debt.

The heavy and perpetual indebtedness forced the cultivators to sell their property to the money-lenders or landlords. Maddox stated in 1900. "There is a reason to fear that in the course of the next thirty years the occupancy right will lapse to a large extent, and thus the Zamindars, who are already purchasing holdings in a considerable quantity will be in possession of an area of *Nij-chas* land much in excess of that which they now hold."[13]

The Emergence of Landless Agricultural Labourers

The cumulative result of the above factors led to the emergence of landless agricultural labourers. The condition of the landless class was most pitiable. They constitute 10% of the population of Orissa. Many of them borrowed at the time of distress. As they had no land to sell, they offered to repay by personal services. They were employed by Zamindars or Mahazans as servants and labourers. The remained in a condition of semi-slavery.[14]

The perpetual scarcity forced many of them top leave for Calcutta in search of employment. The census report 1901 has also observed that, "In a country like India, where two-thirds of the people depended on agriculture, crop failure of natural calamities led the peasants to ruin. The persons mainly affected by famine are the landless labourers.

The labouring classes live from hand to mouth and on the advent of famine are deprived of the means of employment on which they chiefly depend. Whenever, there was scarcity or famine in Bengal presidency, the arkatis could recruit a sufficient number of labourers from Bengal Presidency. Thus, during the highest proportion of recruits were draw from Bengal and mainly from Cuttack, Midnapur, Bankura etc., where the scarcity and famine prevailed.[15]

Condition of Agricultural Labour in South Orissa

Upto the year 1936, the South Orissa comprising Ganjam and Koraput formed a part of the Madras presidency. The Britishers conquered Orissa piece meal manner by 1803 and kept politically divided under three provinces. The Orissa division consisting of the coastal districts of Cuttack, Baleswar and Puri were under Bengal Presidency. Ganjam and Visakhapatnam districts in Madras presidency and Sambalpur district was under central province. Because of this political arrangement, Orissa faced disastrous impact in the living conditions of agricultural community as they were discriminated in socio-economic and educational well-being.

The districts of Ganjam and Koraput were the northern most districts of the Madras presidency which formed presently, the south Orissa. The major portion of South Orissa was mainly inhabited by the tribals who proved to be rebellious. The British Government found it difficult to control them. This factor obstructed the introduction of efficient system of administration and as a result, received inadequate attention by the Madras Government. It appeared as if south Orissa was ruled by the Britishers solely for the purpose of revenue. The economic and educational development of South Orissa was utterly neglected causing pauperisation of the agricultural community.

Thus, it is seen that even though the British government could establish a settled administration in the coastal districts of Cuttack, Puri, and Baleswar, it could not accomplish so in the tribal districts of Ganjam and Koraput.

Agency Administration

The hill Zamindars were known as *Muthadars*. Under them there were Mutha-head and their Subordinates. The income of these Muthadars, Mutha-heads and others were partly paid as 'Mammols'.

The hill Chiefs or *Muthadars* never stayed in their locality and also never frequently visit. The land was left entirely to the Mutha-heads who were known as *Patra*, *Bissoyi*, *Nayak* etc. They owned extensive lands which the *Adivasis* had to Cultivate free of remuneration on 'Bethi' or forced labour system.[16]

The *Adivasis* who were tribal agricultural labourers had to supply *paiks* to carry *daks* from station to station to supervise road and building works, to provide watchers for the government officers, and to collect labourers to carry luggage of the offices on tour.[17]

The Mamool System

In the Kandh agency, the Mamools were not very exorbitant but towards the South Mamools were increasingly found, which was known as *Bethi* system. It has been reported that the *Paik* used to plunder an Adivasi village which he visited. If the *Adivasi* didn't give him some rations or vegetables, he would snatch away whatever he could lay in his hands upon. This mamool system inflicted a green hardship on the Adivasis.[18]

As has been observed form various reports that because of the exploitation inherent in the mamool system and exploitation through the traders/Mahajans of the plains, the tribal agriculturists were impoverished.[19]

The extreme poverty forced many tribal Agricultural labourers to sell or mortgage their lands to the people of the plains. In order to put a full stop to such alienation, the agency tracts land transfer act of 1917 was passed prohibiting all transfer form hill man to non-hill man without express permission of authorities.[20]

The Vetty System of Agricultural Labour

The Royal proclamation of 1846, had considered that vetty labour was one of the wages by which the state was being compensated for the loss of low revenue from the Khands.[21]

Multifarious disadvantages have been found in the vetty system. Vethis (those who perform Vetty labour) were not professional labourers. The work performed by them were not up to the mark. The system discouraged the formation of regular labour class. It prohibited the aborigine to adopt their own avocations according to any programme. Private Vetty had more serious and detrimental effects because, in addition to the evils already explained it had an unfortunate effect in keeping the aborigine always under the inferiority complex.

Gothi System

The continued exploitation of tribal agricultural labourers under the manual system led to widespread poverty among the tribal peasants. In turn, it gave birth to a heinous system known as *Gothi*. This system practically reduced the tribal agricultural labourers to level of serfs, and they spend their lives in a condition of poverty. Even if a Gothi did succeed in repaying of his debt, he was often unable to stand in his own legs and found no alternative but to pledge his services again. Thus, the *gothis* system fell heavily/cruelly and oppressively on the

Gothi labourers. They were left to the mercies of the money lenders or sawcars who exploited them to the unsustainable limit.

Bethi System

Another evil practice which more or less prevailed in all feudal economic systems was a system of *Bethi* or forced labour. Like *Gothi* system it was a native to the soil of the hill districts of Koraput, Ganjam of South Orissa. The Ryot or tenant of the hill tracts of South Orissa would not condensed to labour for a daily wage. In fact, there was no such thing as a labouring class, in the sense of a class of people who voluntarily offered to work for wages.[22]

Forced and Free Labour

This system was resorted to by certain Government officials like rent collectors, Naiks or village headmen. Under the system, the tribal farmers were supplying fuel to police officials, cleaning grass in the station compound without receiving any wages some estate officials used to engage collies for their domestic purposes and paid nothing to them. On the occasion of car festival some villagers were required to cut and carry timber from long distances without any wages.

The Gudam System

It was a system peculiar to certain parts of Koraput district. Under the system, with a nominal value payment in advance, the officials can purchase various agricultural goods and thatching materials. The delivery of goods as a long distance with a fraction of the actual price caused great hardship to the tribal agriculturists. It was mostly prevalent in certain parts of Baipariguda, Thana of Jeypore Taluka and certain other parts of Malkangiri. It was found that mostly the subordinate officials of the state used to advance to the people only a paltry amount for pulses, thatching straw grass, fuel, ghee, and other things and collect worth four or five times the money advanced. The contractors of the PWD used to enter into petty contracts with the village headman who got portions of work executed with the help of their tribal labourers and received payments for the work from the contractor. These village men made profits themselves but did not pay the tribal labourers adequately. The labourers got a fraction of their fair wages and were a victim of the Gudam system.[23]

A perusal of the aforesaid analysis brought to light that because of the backwardness of agriculture, the decay of industry, arbitrary and burdensome taxation, the imposition of varieties of cesses, illegal extraction, *Bethi*, the apathy of the Britishers, erratic behaviour of monsoon, all these led to the perpetual poverty of the tribal agricultural labourers in Orissa.

Growth of Poverty

Several factors accounted for the growth of poverty among the agricultural labourers in Orissa. The extreme poverty among the tribal agriculture was main occupation of the labouring class people it was in the state of stagnation and deterioration.[24] Over crowing of agriculture, result in sub-division and small holding, low productivity and unemployment. The abject poverty of the overwhelming majority of the agricultural labourers left them without any resources with which to improve agriculture by using better cattle, seeds, fertiliser etc.

The assessment of land revenue by the British government was not only heavy but also extremely harassing to the agriculturists due to the rigid manner of collection. The system of *Bethi* or forced labour was not only demoralising to the agricultural labourers but also causing them much economic distress.

The tribal areas of Orissa, were mainly consists of backward tribals like *Khandas, Sabour, Boda, Poraja, Gohds, Mattiyas* etc. Most of them were agriculturists but their ignorance, impoverished conditions, extreme climatic conditions and mountain barriers kept them isolated from the mainstream of the economy.[25] The supplemented their income partly by labour and partly by collecting fruits and forest products. However, due to occurrence of flood, drought and heavy rent and poverty of agricultural labourers there was enormous rise in prices of food grains which consequently, assigned the labouring classes. The forced labour system, *Gothi, Betty-all* led to landless agricultural labourers. The able bodiedmen immigrated to Burma or elsewhere at comparatively little cost to eke-out their living. This has been evidently clear from the report of the Whitley Commission. The commission observed that, Oriya workers used to go to Rangoon, Assam, Bengal and Bombay in order to serve in plantation, earth work, dams, roads, railways, jute mils, textile mills, etc. because of chronic effects of famine and flood and the economic condition of the people, pressure of population on land decay of industries, exploitation by the feudal lords (princely States).[26]

Conclusion

The analysis brings into light that owing to historical causes, Orissa, remained exploited and under-developed for a long period of time. The backwardness of agriculture, the increasing dependence of the people on agriculture, complete neglect of industrialisation, excessive land revenue, the exploitation of the poor peasants by the Zamindars and money lenders reduced the people of Orissa to extreme poverty. The land alienation, indebtedness, lack of irrigation and callous attitude of the Government, recurring drought and failure of crops, dominance of tribal and weaker sections—all contributed to the emergence of landless agricultural labourers in Orissa.

In the tribal regions, the Britishers adopted the policy of non-interference and isolation. Thus, because of apathetic policy, the organisation capabilities of the tribal turners were destroyed. Thus, wide-spread poverty, ignorance and exploitation of Farmers were the marked characteristics of British rule in India.

References

1. Jena, K.C., Land Revenue Administration in Orissa, S. Chand and Co., New Delhi, 1968, pp. 213–214.
2. Madox Report, Vol. 1, p. 172.
3. Jena, K.C., Land Revenue Administration in Orissa, *Op. cit.*, p. 216.
4. Mukherjee, P., History of Orissa during 19th Century, p. 357.
5. Jena, K.C., Land Revenue Administration in Orissa, *Op. cit.* p. 222.
6. Report on Suppression of human sacrifice and female infanticide, pp. 2–5.
7. Quinquennial Administration Report, Orissa, 1900–01 to 1904–05, p. .7.
8. Report on the Administration of Bengal (Bengal Presidency) 1901–1902, p. 49.
9. Patnaik, Gorachand, The famine and some aspects of the British Economic Policy in Orissa, 1806–1905, Vidyapuri, Cuttack, 1980, p. 188.
10. Samal, J. K., Orissa under the British Crown 1858–1905, S. Chand and Company Ltd., New Delhi., p. 361.
11. Maddox, S. L., *Report*, Volume–II, p. 490.

12. Maddox, S.L., *Report,* Volume–II, p. 491. Quoted in "Orissa under the British Crown" by J. K. Samal.
13. Maddox, S. L., Reports–II, p. 493.
14. The *Census Report* 1901, Government of India, pp. 85–86.
15. Report of the Administration Enquiry Committee, 1958, Vol. 1, p. 9.
16. Report of the Muthahead Abolition Committee, Cuttack 1970 pp. 9.
17. Report of the Administration Enquiry Committee, 1958, Vol. 1, pp. 31–32.
18. Taylor, H.D., Memoir on the Ganjam Maliaha in the Madras Presidency, Madras, p. 10.
19. Report of the Administrative Enquiry Committee, Vol. 1, 1958. pp. 461–462.
20. *Ibid.*, p. 29–30.
21. Apat, Sontosh Kumar, British Economic Policy in South Orissa, 1858–1936 (Unpublished Ph.D. Thesis) Berhampur University, 1989 p. 158.
22. Behuria, N.C., Final Report on the mahor Settlement Operation in Koraput District, 1938–1964, Cuttack (1966), pp. 43–44.
23. Apat, Santosh Kumar, British Economic Policy in South Orissa, Op. cit., p. 223.
24. Bailey, F.G., Caste and Economic Frontier (A Village in Highland Orissa), Oxford University Press, 1962, p. 19.
25. Royal Commission on Labour, (1931), pp. 11, 426, 429, 439.

3
Socio-Economic Problems of Contractual Agricultural Labourers

This Chapter attempts to portray the trend and growth of agricultural labour in India with special reference to study area. The problem of contractual labour manifested in the sample village and their socio-economic problems have also been outlined.

Labourers in agricultural sectors are distributed into three main categories : (i) Cultivators, (ii) agricultural labourers, and labourers engaged in forestry fishing and live stock etc. The National Commission on labour defined an agricultural labourer as one who earns his income by wage employment and who are generally unskilled and unorganised. Thus, the landless agricultural labourers, small farmers and marginally farmer are also included in the purview of agricultural labourers.

Work Force/Employment

Labour being a primary factor of production, the size of labour force is of great significance for the level of economic activity in a country. In the determination of the size of the labour force, it is customary to exclude children below the age of 15 and old people above the age of 60, although in our country, poverty constrains people belonging to these groups also to work for bare subsistence. The work force participation rose in our country implies the proposition of working population to total population.

Labour Force

Against the static nation of work force/employment that censuses adopted in terms of stable (or 'usual') activity patterns, the NSS rounds in employment and unemployment followed the labour force approach. Conforming theoretically to full employment situation, this approach considers various in the levels of employment over shorter intervals. The population is divided into three categories :

i) The employed, reporting gainful activity over the (short) reference period such as 'one week'.

ii) The unemployment, not so engaged but are actively seeking work (in later rounds amended to include those who may not be actively seeking work, but are available for work), and

iii) Persons not in the full labour force.

Thus, labour force includes those currently unemployed unlike the census categories which divide the population into two categories—'workers' and 'non-workers' on the basis of stable activity patterns over the plus side, the NSS approach seems to capture the seasonal element in rural employment through its method of sub-rounds and in some sense also included the irregular or casual nature of employment by introducing shorter reference periods, the problems essentially remain. For example, construction women labourers who enter into hired labour marked temporarily or occasionally to supplement their household income, may not report themselves to be included in the labour force. This is because their active participation into active work force depends on :

i) the volume of work forthcoming.

ii) condition attached to work like timings, lacking of the work site and their domestic burdens. Thus, this creates problems in the computation of 'labour force participation rates' for females as well as in the aggregate.

However, in the Table 3.1, labour force projection has been made on the basis of seventh plan document of the planning commission.

Table 3.1 : Labour Force Projection (in Million)

Year	*Rural*	*Urban*	*Total*
1980	180.26	51.42	237.68
1985	206.79	63.02	269.81
1990	228.61	77.47	306.08
2000	264.33	115.52	279.85

Source : 7th Plan Document, Planning Commission Economic References, Employment and Poverty Trends and Options.

According to the national commission on rural labour (1991), during 1997–98, out of a total of 108.4 million rural households, 43 million household belonged to rural labour household. Among the rural labour household, agricultural household were to the tune of 33.3 million. In relative terms rural labour household allowed for 39.7 result of total labour household and agriculture labour household were in the order of 30.7 per cent. This shows that agricultural labour household constituted about 77 per cent of all rural labour households in 1987–88.

Increasing Trend of Agricultural Labour

Many studies have indicated the increased trend of the share of agricultural labour households in all rural households. Table 3.2 also shows similar trend. Between 1963–64 and 1983, the number of rural households increased by 49 per cent while date of agricultural labour households increased by more than 100 per cent. The percentage of agricultural labour households in the total rural households increased steadily from around 21 per cent 1963–64 to 31 per cent in 1983.

Table 3.2 : Number of Rural and Agricultural Labour Households : All India

Category of Households	*1963–64*	*1977–78*	*1983–84*
Agricultural Households	67.6	95.7	100.5
Agricultural Labour Households	14.1	28.6	30.9
	(20.9)	(29.9)	(30.6)

Sources : (i) Rural labour enquiry, Final Report (1963–65), Ministry of Labour, Government of India.

(ii) 32nd Round of NSS on employment and unemployment "sarvekshana" Vol. V, Nos. 1 and 2, July–October, 1981.

(iii) 38th Round of NSS, Report on the third Quinquennial Survey on Employment and unemployment, NSS Report No. 341 NSS, Ministry of Planning, Govt. of India (Percentage in the parenthesis refer to the percentage of agricultural households in total rural households).

It has been manifested that the proportion of the wage labour of total works force increased at the all India label from 34.1 per cent in 1972–73 to 41.4 per cent in 1987–88.[1] During the same record, the proportion of the casual labour increased from 66.8 per cent in

1972–73 to 75.8 per cent in 1987–88.[2] Analysing the increasing trend of casualisation of agricultural labour, the National commission on Rural Labour (1991) states; "The technological change in agricultural, marginalisation of small farmers, eviction of tenants, destruction of tradition cottage industries, inflation etc. are some of the important factors they are operating differently in different regions of India leading to the swelling of the member of agricultural labourers".[3]

Casualisation of Rural Labour

The rural work force is increasingly casualised. This is because of the following important reasons.

i) Small farmers cultivating small plots of land are constrained to seek wage employment as a households strategy.

ii) The natural growth of landless agricultural labour itself.

Another indicator of casualisation in the growth of rural labour households as a proportional all rural households.

A close observation of the Table 3.3 reveals that the trend of increase in rural labour households and agricultural labour households is at higher rate than the trend in the increase in the rural households.

Table 3.3 : Trends in Rural Labour and Agricultural Labour Households in India

(*in million*)

Year	*Rural* Households	*Rural* *Labour* Households	Agricultural Labour Households
1974–75 (Second Rural Labour Enquiry)	82.1	24.8	20.7
1977–78 (Third Rural Labour Enquiry)	95.7	32.2	28.6
1983–84 (Fourth Rural Labour Enquiry)	100.5	37.5	30.9
1987–88 (Fifth Rural Labour Enquiry)	108.4	43.8	33.3

Source : Government of India (1991), Report of the National Commission on Rural Labour, Vol. 1, Ministry of Labour, New Delhi.

Table 3.4 unfolds that during the decennial population census of 1981–91 the agricultural labourers increased 55.5 millions to 74.6

millions and thus that increased of 19.1 millions where as during the said period the number of cultivators increased from 92.5 millions to 110.6 million and thus, a net increase of 18.1 millions. This clearly shows that agricultural labourers increased at a rate faster than that of cultivators.

Table 3.4 : Workers and Agricultural Labour (Main All-India)

(*in million*)

Census	*All Workers (Main Workers)*	*Agricultural Labour*	*Cultivators*
1971	180.5	47.5	78.3
1981	222.5	55.5	92.5
1991	255.9	74.6	110.6

Source : Government of India (1991), Report of the National Commission on Rural Labour, Vol. 1, Ministry of Labour, New Delhi.

For deriving the main workers for 1981 and 1991, marginal workers are excluded from the figures.

It is seen from the Table that during 1993–94 there has been increase of casual labour both for male and females. In the context of such an increase trend of agricultural labourers into casual wages labourers, poverty alleviation programmes would need reformulation and changes for better employment and wages to agricultural labours.

Table 3.5 analyses data regarding the percentage rural poverty and extent of unemployment in the selected states of India. As revealed from the table that the percentage of agricultural labours in Andhra Pradesh is the highest (40.9%) followed Bihar and Orissa with 37.1 and 28.7% respectively. The incidence poverty is acute in Orissa among the states under review (57.6%). Bihar occupies second position of rural poverty with 52.6%, while Punjab has the least poverty incidence among the states. The percentage of rural unemployment has been the highest in Orissa both for males and females with 8.8 and 5.4 percentage respectively.

Wage Labour in Agriculture

Freedom of employment, or the freedom of member of the labour force to dispose of a fundamental resource, and one that they each posses, labour power must be regarded as a crucial aspect of economic development. Prof. Ram. Chandran (1990)[4] describes and analyses

Table 3.5 : Rural Poverty and Unemployment in Various States

States	Percentage of Rural Labour (1991)	Poverty (%)	Percentage of Agricultural Rural Unemployed	
			Male	Female
Andhra Pradesh	40.9	20.9	2.5	4.5
Bihar	37.1	52.6	2.6	0.8
Gujrat	22.9	28.7	2.4	1.7
Madhya Pradesh	23.5	41.9	0.9	1.2
Orissa	28.7	57.6	8.8	5.4
Punjab	23.8	12.6	2.9	7.4
Rajasthan	10.0	33.2	3.0	1.8

Source : Data compiled. The Indian Rural Labour Economics, Vol. 40, No. 4, Oct.–December, 1997 p. 775.

the occurrence of production, the form that wage labour forces and other forms of unfreedom and production relations.

As part of its argument regarding wage labour and unfreedom author discuss a range of issues of which contemporary village level data are not always available. These include poverty and inequality among rural households, inter-generational occupation change, demand for labour is irrigated and in irrigated agriculture, employment, unemployment and seasonality of employment wages and indebtedness and aspects of labour process in agriculture.

Contractual Labour

Needless to mention that there is a human element involved in case of labour. Therefore, the labour market cannot be equalised with that of the market for capital or commodity. Moreover, the conversion of labour power into a commodity presupposes that its owner has been free from personal bondage. The various types of contractual arrangement in agriculture labour market have been explored along with rationale for their operation (Sarap, 1992).[5]

The neo-marxian school try to explain institution of contractual arrangement on the basis of ownership structure of means of production and poverty relations. The local label power structure determines the contractual arrangements, viz., duration, type of work and wage to a great extent (Rudar, 1984).[6]

The Study

The present study has been made in 4 village of Ganjam district through personal interview method with the help of a structured questionnaire. During the field survey, the researcher endeavoured to collect information about the number of landless labourers, employment opportunities available, the wage rate prevailed during the time of survey for different form activities for both male and female agriculture labourers. Thus, information is both relevant and useful as it gives a broad picture on the system of contractual labour in agricultural sector of Orissa.

Ganjam district covered an area of 12,5365 square kilometers, out of 4,698 villages, 4265 villages are inhabited and 433 villages are uninhabited, divided into 14 tehsils. There are 466 Gram Panchayats under 29 blocks and 4 sub-divisions. In urban set-up, there are two municipalities and 18 notified areas councils in the district.

According to 1991 census, there are 31,42,120 population in the district out of which 26,02,714 (82.18%) population reside in villages. The scheduled caste and scheduled tribe population constitute about 12.76 per cent and 8.05 per cent respectively of the total population. Agriculture is the main thrust of the economy, but of the rural main workers, there are 39 thousand (42.13 per cent) cultivators, and 30 thousand (32.4 per cent) agriculture labourers who depend in it.

Out of the rural 29 blocks undivided Ganjam district, two blocks have been randomly selected. For selection of villages from Aska and Digapahandi blocks, simple random sampling method has been used.

The Data and General Characteristics of Sample Villages

Before we analyse the field data it is imperative to focus some light on the characteristic of sample villages. Because, the nature of the village economy, the level of development in rural areas have some influence in determining the system of labour in existence and other related issues.

Bijepadmanapur

It is known as ladigam in this locality and situated 5 kms. away from Digapahandi block towards east-south corner and in revenue records it is known as Bigepadmanavpur. The rural geographical area of the village is 22.946 hectors. There are 231 households in the village. This is mainly a paddy growing area. Around 3/4th of the cultivating area depend upon tank irrigation which in turn depend upon intensity of rain.

Khamarigam

This village is located 16 kms. away from the Digapahandi block. The total geographical are of village is 204.77 hector as for revenue records. There are 162 households living in the village during the period of survey. The inhabitants of the village are mainly engaged in agricultural activities. The Ghodahada dam irrigated most of the land and therefore, rice and other vegetables like banana, various flowers are extensively grown in the region.

K. Bangarada

This is the hamlet village of Khukundia located 17 kms. away from Aska block headquarters towards North. The total geographical area of village is 645.07 hectors. Rice and paddy are the principal agricultural product of the village.

Mangalpur

The village Mangalpur has the total geographical area of 466.77 hectors, situated 5 kms. away from Aska block headquarters. There are 370 households in the village during the period of survey.

In this four villages of Aska and Digapahandi of Ganjam district, first of all survey was made to find out contractual labourers for intensive study.

Contractual labourers are known as farm servant or Halia in the district of Ganjam. They are more or less in continuous employments. The contact of the employees are informal, oral and personalise. The duration of contact is mostly for one year; but contracts more than one year also observed.* The mode of payment (wage) is either both

---

* Dolpurnima is the date fix for appointment and termination of contract labour or halia by the landlords. There are usually hired on a yearly contract, renewable at the end of the contract. They may, however, be contractor for specific seasons or less than one year contract which are not uncommon. The practice of hiring permanent of contract labours, especially by the large land owners is allowed to be hedge against the risk of not finding and ensured supply of labour during seasonal peasants agricultural production. This is a mutual feature in the employer-employee relationship, since the workers especially when he is landless, could be assured of a year's employment and earnings.

monthly and yearly in kind, or monthly payment in kind or case. The wage rate is higher in urban areas then in rural areas because of high demand of labourers in urban land holdings.

The annual payment ranges 450 to 500 kgs. of rice. In addition to that, they are also supplied free meals once in a day. The salary increases year to year at the rate of usually·10 per cent depending upon the range of price like. These generally perfomed 8–12 hours of work in a day.

During off season they are employed in animal rearing, household works, construction of house work and other works, as directed by the employer. In the peak season, if the contract labour remains deliberately absent in his works he is thrown out of his job.

Sometimes, when the contact labourer is victimised by disease or health hazards he fails to arrange money. Generally, households with large family size remain in the grip of such problems and they join in the institution of halia or contract labour system. The permanent labour employed usually for a year has to do various types of works like land reclamation, fencing, sugar cane collection, even do work in the lands situated 4/5 kms. away from the native village.

The income of the contract labour is limited due to restricted scope of employment. In case of heavy financial crisis, it becomes unmanageable on the part of the halia to tide over the crisis.

If the halia remains absent for two to three months due to sickness, the employer engages labourers on daily wage basis and makes some deduction from the salary of the halia. Generally, the exact amount is not deducted but some relaxation is allowed.

Trust and mutual understanding is the corner stone of this contractual labour system.

In recent years, the enactments like contract Labour Abolition Act and Bonded Labour Abolition Act, 1976 has led to the percentage decline in halia system.

Dr. Sundram[7] has observed that the attached labour households which constituted 9.7 per cent of the total agricultural labour households in 1950–51 had increase to 26.63% by the end of the sixties. Capitalism in Indian agriculture is fast expanding but the relationship between farmers and labourers continues to be semi-feudal in most part of the country.

As has been mentioned earlier, short term contact for 2/3 months or for 5/7 days may also be made by the employer during the peak season for assumed supply of agricultural labour.

Attached labourers are also in the same category of contract labour. The wages generally paid to the attached or contract labourers have been presented in the Table 3.6, based on field enquiry.

Table 3.6 : Labour Contracts and Payments in Orissa

Sl. No.	*Farm Activity*	*Payment per Acre (in Rs.)*	*Number of Labour*		*Commission of the labour contractor per contract*
			Male (wage rate) (in Rs.)	*Female (wage rage) (in Rs.)*	
1.	Transplantation	600	5(40)	10(30)	100
2.	Harvesting	550	4(35)	10(30)	110
3.	Harvesting and Binding	700	4(50)	10(40)	100
4.	Threshing, winnowing and cleaning	800	8(60)	5(40)	120

Source : Field study conducted in Ganjam District (Orissa).

The Table reveals that the extent of commission increases with the increase in the farm activity. The middleman or contractor receives comparatively more commission at the time of harvesting than at the time of transplantation. The Table further unfolds the fact that the wage rate of both male and female agricultural labourers increase with the increase in working hours. Where as in transplantation work more female labourers are employed but in threshing, winnowing and cleaning operation the number of male agricultural labourers are comparatively more.

However, it is found that in all agricultural operations, the females receive comparatively lower wages than their male counterparts.

An army of cultivators depending on small and sub-divided holdings better termed as subsistence farmers have been classified as 'cultivators' in the census reports but in reality they are agricultural labourers. Landless labourers belonging to other category are without family enterprise solely depend upon wage-period employment or alternatively called casual manual labour. They are not 'wage labour' as their casualisation in the labour market is not accompanied by a sustained demand for their labour.

Casual Labourers

Casual labour is that type of hired labour which is usually hired on a day to day basis, sometimes for less than a day although the casual worker may have to work for a continuous number of days for various crop operations. The wages of casual labourers are paid on a daily basis, including a cash and a kind (especially meals) component.

Casual labour constitutes the most pervasive form of hired labour.

The wage payment to the casual labourer for various agricultural operating have been depicted in the Table 3.7 which clearly indicates the discriminatory wage payments to the females.

Table 3.7 : Wage Structure for Casual Labourers for Different Agricultural Operations

Major Farm Operation	*Male*	*Female*	*Children*
Showing and transplanting	35	25	15
Threshing	35	25	15
Harvesting	35	25	15
Ploughing	35	—	—

Source : Collected from field Survey.

The interview schedule contained questionnaire relating to land-holding position of the rural households, their terms of employment and use of labour in agricultural operations, payment of wages etc. Using the data on the family labour disposition an attempt was made to classify broadly the payments in the sample villages in the 3 classes. These classes are :

(i) the big farmer (land-lord) (BF)

(ii) the middle peasant (MP)

(iii) the marginal farmers and landless agricultural labourers (MF & LA).

The important features of the classification are as follows :

A big farmer is one who does not perform any physical labour of cultivating the land personally but do supervise the production process. He too employ contract labourers and casual labourers (during peak season).

A middle peasant is considered as a person who engage himself as well as his family members in the agricultural operations. He may not employ permanent contact labourer but usually employ casual labourers. During peak season, he also employs for a short period agricultural labourers on contact basis for certain agricultural operations like transplantation, harvesting, etc.

The marginal farmers and landless labourers are those who do not employ either contact or casual labourers. The family members of such peasants perform their physical labour in their marginal land holding as well as in the agricultural operations of other people for earning wages. Such category of farmers one in the last rung of the ladder, an economically in the distressed conditions.

In our total 4 sample villages, the total number of rural households were 1071, out of which the aforesaid categories of agricultural peasants and labourers were found only in 742 households.

The detailed study of different categories of households have been made in the following tables, followed by their analysis.

Table 3.8 and 3.9 provide the details of the distribution of households according to their social classes and the involvement of the families in the sale and purchase of labour in the labour market. From the Table 3.8 it is noticed that out of 742 households 166 households belonged to big farmers (BF) and 124 households belong

Table 3.8 : Sale of Labour According to Social Group

Category of Households	*No. of Households*	*No. of family sales labour (casual)*	*No. of family sales labour (attached or contract*	*No. of family sales labour outside agriculture*
BF	116	—	—	—
MP	124	—	—	27
MF & LA	502	342	35	118
Total	742	354	35	145

Table 3.9 : Purchase of Labour According to Social Group

Category of House-holds	*No. of House-holds*	*No. of family works as supervisor only*	*No. of family directly participate in agri-culture*	*No. of family purchase casual labour*	*No. of family purchase contract labour*
BF	116	116	26	116	35
MP	124	05	124	110	05
MF & LA	502	—	140	—	—
Total	742	—	490	226	40

to middle peasants (MP) group who do not sell labour their labour to any other peasants. However, out of 124 middle peasants, households 27 families constituting 21.7 per cent sell their labour outside agriculture. They were formed migrating to other places to earn more income.

Moreover, there are 502 families in the group of marginal farmers and landless agricultural labourers (AL & LA) marginal farmers are those who possess less than half an area of land, and the actual number of families belonging to this category is 140. The rest 362 households are landless agricultural labourers. Some of them had land holding but gradually due to their poverty and indebtedness lost their land-holding. Probably the big farmers or the middle peasants purchased their small holdings. However, we have taken altogether the both types of households *i.e.* the marginal farmer families and landless labour households into a group, which comes to 502 households. Thus, out of 502 households, 342 households have reported their selling of labour as casual labourers in the labour market. In percentage term, more than 68% of families have been selling their service as casual labourers. Even 35 families constituting about seven per cent of the families have reported working as attached or contract labour.

Thus, altogether 75% of this MF & LA group sale their labour both as casual and attached/contract labour in the labour market. It is also demonstrated from the Table 3.8, that 118 households *i.e.* 23.5% of the total households have been selling their labour outside the agriculture. It is implied that 118 families have reported about their migrant work men working in various project-sites situated in the neighbouring states or mostly at Surat (Gujrat). Thus, it is informed that MF & LA is the single largest group who sell their labour in the labour market either as casual or contact labour or both casual and migrant labour.

Explaining about the purchase of labour by different social group, Table 3.9 unfolds that all must be all 116 BF group families perform supervisory work and mainly depend on casual labourers. However, there are 26 households who reported that they do participate in various agricultural operations. In addition to the purchase of casual labour, about 35 households have also reported using contact labour.

Similarly, in the group of 124 middle peasants, families reported using casual labour which is more than 88% of the total families.

Only five families home reported using attached or contract labour. From among the 502 MF & LA group, almost all marginal farmer families (140) directly participate in agriculture. In this group, no household has reported about purchase of either casual or contract labour for agricultural operations.

Thus, it is revealed from the analysis that only a total of 40 households out of 742 households used contract labour (5.3 per cent of the total).

Table 3.10 depicts data on distribution of households producing different crops according to social groups. It is revealed that the principal crop grown in the sample villages is paddy, followed by sugar cane. Only a total of 83 families reported cultivating vegetables of which 62 families i.e. 74.6% families belonged to MF & LA group. Because, two of the sample villages belonged to Aska block, where Aska Corporation Sugar factory has been located, the farmers are encouraged to grow sugar cane. Thus, a total of 77 households have reported about sugar cane cultivation.

Table 3.10 : Distribution of Households Producing Various Crops

Category of Households	*No. of Households*	*Number of Family Cultivating*		
		Paddy	*Sugarcane*	*Vegetables*
BF	116	67	39	10
MP	124	75	38	11
MF & LA	502	78	—	62
Total	**742**	**220**	**77**	**83**

Consumer durables owned by various social groups have been analysed in the Table 3.11. The Table shows that in the possession of consumer durables the big farmer group occupies the distinctive position. In this group, all most all families house watch, 85 households house television set, 82 households have radio and 38 reported having vehicles. Some of them have reported having all the consumer durable. Fifty percent of the households have T.V. set in the MP group where as 70 families house cycles. In the distribution of consumer durables the MF and LA group occupies the lowest position. Only 2 families reported having TV sets, 26 families having cycle, four families having radio and not a single family possessing vehicle.

Table 3.11 : Consumer Durable Owned by Different Social Groups

Category of House-holds	*No. of House-holds*	*Consumers' Durable Owned*				
		Cycle	*Radio*	*Vehicle*	*Watch*	*T.V.*
BF	116	82	48	38	116	85
MP	124	70	46	25	106	62
MF & LA	502	26	04	—	12	02
Total	**742**	**178**	**98**	**63**	**334**	**149**

The indebted position of the rural households have been examined in the Table 3.12. Generally, a loan may be contracted and utilised for producting, or it may be used exclusively for satisfying immediate economic needs or to discharge religious/social obligations. The latter aspect is always viewed with alarm by the economists and the policy makers. Rural labouring class in India mainly fall prey to

Table 3.12 : Distribution of Debt among the Social Groups

Category of House-holds	*No. of House-holds*	*No. of Family in Debt*	*Sources of Debt*		*Mode of Debt*	
			Institu-tional	*Non-institu-tional*	*Cash*	*Kind*
BF	116	92	92	—	92	—
MP	124	66	52	14	66	—
MF & LA	502	108	40	68	76	32
Total	**742**	**266**	**184**	**82**	**234**	**32**

the malaise of indebtedness on account of the gap in the insufficient income and the inescapable consumption expenditure. Consequently, this class has no option but to contact loans for non-productive purposes. In our analysis, 92 households, constituting mere than 73%, in the group of BF class have reported their indebtedness from Canara Bank or from Rushikulya Gramya Bank for buying agricultural implements, tractors and other needs. More than 53% families constituting 66 households in the MP group have been indebted both from institutional and non-institutional sources. In the above two categories loans where mainly taken in cash. Only 108 household among 502 households in the MF & LA group have been indebted which is 21.5 per cent of the total. It is interesting to note that out of 108 indebted families only 40 families were indebted from institutional source where as 68 households have borrowed from non-institutional sources finance mainly to this category. Again, loans sanctioned to this group by institutional source is the least. This shows that in the institutional finance to the BF and MP group are the privileged group. Thus, the institutional finance is not in favour of marginal farmers and landless labourer. This probably due to the fact that they do not have required security or the repayment capacity or the purpose of loan may be for unproductive purpose. Only 32 households in the group MF & LA availed loans through kind. No other class have reported available loans in kinds.

A persual of our discussion brings into light that casual labourers enjoy better freedom and scope of employment compared to contractual labourers in the agricultural sector in Orissa.

The marginal farmers and landless agricultural labour (MF & LA) in the single larger group who sell their labour in the labour market as casual or contract labour or both casual and migrant labour. Only a meagre per cent of 5.3% households use contract or attached labour.

The principal crop grown in the sample villages is paddy, followed by sugar cane.

In the distribution of consumer durables the MF and LA group occupies the coyest position.

Institutional finance is available more to higher income or landed aristocracy than the marginal farmers and landless labourers. Credit from institutional sources flow mere than 73% to the social class of BF and MP where as the MF and LA group receive only a limited percentage 21.5 per cent.

Except the MF & LA group no other class available loan in kind.

Thus, the contract labour originates from among the marginal farmers and landless agricultural labourers who actually sell permanently their services to the big farmers (BF).

References

1. Dutt, Ruddar and Sundaram, K.P.M., Indian Economy, S. Chand & Co. Ltd., New Delhi (1997), p. 544.
2. *Ibid.*
3. Ministry of Labour, Report of the National Commission on Labour (1991). Vol. 1, p. 59.
4. Ramachandran, V.K., Wage Labour and Unfreedom in agriculture : An Indian Case Study. Clarendian Press, Oxford (1990).
5. Sarap, K., Changing Contractual Arrangements in Agricultural Labour Market : Evidence from Orissa. Economic and Political Weekly, 26(52) A-167-A-177 (1992).
6. Rudra, A., "Local Power and Farm-Level Decision Making" in Desai, Rudolph and Rudra edited Arragrian Power and Agricultural Productivity in South Asia, Delhi, Oxford University Press (1984).
7. Satya, Sundram, I (Dr.), Rural Development, Himalaya Publishing House, Mumbai (1997), p. 198.

4

Concluding Observations and Policy Implications of the Study

This chapter deals with the summary conclusions and findings of all the chapters covered in the study. In addition, this chapter also delineates some policy suggestions.

Orissa for a long period remained exploited and underdeveloped because of historical factors. The Orissan people were in the lowest rung of the ladder owing to backwardness of agriculture, delay of industries, and exorbitant land revenue policy adopted by Britishers. The land alienation, indebtedness and exploitation by the traders and mahajans, lake of irrigation, apathy of the Government, frequent drought and flood are some of the factors responsible for backwardness of rural people.

As the total income from agricultural sector is inadequate to meet their consumption requirements of agricultural labours they are compelled to work in construction activities, forest collections, stone breaking and even work in near by and distant places. It has been revealed from the interview schedules that the principal factors for labour migration from rural to urban in our study are :

(i) Lack of employment and lower wages rate in rural sector.

(ii) Comparatively higher scope of employment in urban areas, construction or service sector with a relatively higher wage rate, supplied by contractors or concerned employer than the wage offered by medium or large land owners in rural areas.

This may be due to the fact that labour supply is comparatively higher in rural sector than in urban sector. The landless and marginal farmers migrate to urban sector in order to meet the higher express due to price like which they confront in the rural sector. There are 118 households out of 502 households in our study do migrate for maintaining their livelihood as well as for better earnings (Table 3.8).

Casual labourers enjoy better freedom and scope of complimentary compared to contractual labours in the agricultural sector of Orissa.

The marginal farmers and landless agricultural labours (MF and LA) is the single largest group who sell their labour in the labour market as casual or contract labours or contract labour or both casual and migrant labours.

In the distribution of consumer durables, the MF & LA group occupies the lowest position.

Industrial finance flows were to the higher landed aristocracy to marginal farmers and landless labourers.

Thus, the contract labourers or attached labours do originate from among the marginal farmers and landless agricultural labourers who are employed by the big farmers (BF).

The central theme of the issue of agricultural labourers at this critical stage of agricultural development, evolution of property as well as social relations in rural villages is the organisation and bargaining strength of the agricultural labours.

In the absence of organisation and bargaining power, the agricultural labours are in capable to get justifiable and reasonable reward for their labour through collective bargaining. The repressive organs of the state in the rural areas, which have close links, economic and social, with the rich and middle peasantry reinforce the violent methods against the landless agricultural labourers and poor peasantry.

The planning commission recommended in the second five year plan specially treatment to the group of the labourers covered under contract labour. It suggested that in the case of contract labour the major problem related to the regulation of their working conditions and ensuring them continuous employment. The planning commission realised that it was necessary to secure for contract labour the conditions and protection enjoyed by other workers engaged by principal employer, and set-up a scheme of decasualisation, whenever feasible.

But, it is lamentable that there has been steadily decline of the real wage of agricultural labours after 1960–61 despite increases in agricultural production and improvement in the terms of trade and procurement prices for agricultural produce. It is observed that the grains of production and productivity in agricultural sector have been monopolised by the landed interests.

In this context the role minimum wages legislators has its importance. The fixation of minimum wages under the statute, can be useful only if the wage levels so fixed are above the prevailing level established by customs. But in reality, wages prescribed under the minimum wages laws are usually fixed below the prevailing wages. There is also no effective machinery enforcement of the minimum wages.

The act has not been implemented properly as depicted the levels of actual wages and earnings of Agricultural labourers (Ghanekar, 1997) (Tripathy, 1997). The National Commission on rural labours (Goi, 1991) has also reflected similar opinion. The commission has observed that the statutory minimum wages has not been paid to agricultural labourers expect in states Kerala, Punjab and Haryana. The minimum wages in Orissa were revised on four occasions during the period 1982 to 1990 as compared to 7 such revisions during the period of 1954 to 1981. According to the latest revision done in 1990 the minimum wages were revised from Rs. 12 per day to Rs. 25 per day.

The enforcement efforts lacked effectiveness inspite of the involvement of the officers of the revenue department.

In view of the substantial high-wages-employment in building operations, tiles and brick making activities, the wages levels in agriculture is pushed up to a higher level compared to the wage levels exists in backward tribal regions of other states. The labourers as well as the employers in the villagers covered in the study area were mostly conscious of the minimum wages act and equal remuneration laws, but the details of the laws and about the wage revisions they had a sketchy idea.

The study revealed that in some villages the employers have a tendency to substitute the hired labour by personal or family labour. Because of the growing cost of hired labour, some also prefer to annual contract labour.

The enforcement machinery did not have adequate resources

implementing the Minimum Wages Act, 1948 in the widely scattered and poorly contacted villages all over the district and the state.

The inspecting officials have their genuine difficulties in perusing the case of non-payment of minimum wages for many of farm lands due to lack of reliable evidence from the poor, ignorant and illiterate labourers.

The relative backwardness of females, tribals, untouchables, and economically as well as culturally retarded caste groups who own no other productive resources except their labour services should be provided with some basic services through public welfare expenditures. 'Such expenditures may increase their productive potential, and also their consumer satisfaction in terms of health, education, communication etc. tend to alter productivity and are thus, essentially capital investment in human resources.

Rural development schemes and financial allocations for these schemes during five year plans tend to dilute their significance unless they are associated with the benefits of improving the bargaining power of agricultural labours in the villages so that they embark upon struggle against the exploiters of their labour.

It goes without saying that agricultural households are among the poorest segments of the rural society. Their principal source of livelihood is wage employment. The income of such households are to inadequate to support their bare necessity of life. The earning of such household can be increased by :

(i) Raising their wages,

(ii) Increasing the total days of employment.

(iii) Improving the productivity of their existing assets, and

(iv) Creation of new assets.

The poverty amelioration programmes like Integrated Rural Development Programme (I.R.D.P.), National Rural Employment Programme (NREP), Jawahar Rojgar Yojana (JRY) which are aimed at alleviating the poverty condition of targets group are important but inadequate to tackle the magnitude of the problem.

Prof. Dandeker (1986) has apply remarked, "the size of problem is simple too large as compared to the size of the anti-poverty programmes".

As revealed from over study that Agricultural labourers are in the grip of acute underemployment, scattered nature of work place, no unionisation and lack of relationship between employer employee. The unrecognised agriculture workers are unprotected due to lack of trade unions and suitable legislation to cover such labours.

Regarding the unorganised agriculture labourers has to be wade through the elimination of exploitation with the active support of the NGOs and the trade unions. Co-operatives can emerge as democratic institutions which promote self-help through self-management.

The recommendations of national commission or rural labour, control integration for agricultural labour provision of institutional arrangements for consumption of unorganised rural labour in general, under social security umbrellas in all form of both insurance based and government schemes like old age revision and maternity benefits, deserve immediate attention.

The rural power structure and rural labours relations, are to be changed alongwith appropriate legislations. The terminal security is to be guaranteed with a view to preventing the eviction of small and marginal farmers.

Since the dawn of planning in India, agricultural sector has been supporting and maintaining the food requirements of teeming millions of India. The pressure of population has rapidly increased resulting in unemployed mass. The non-agricultural sector could not succeeded in absorbing the mounting unemployed and thus, in view of privatisation and globalization policy mainly applicable to non-agricultural sector, the agricultural sector is the only sector to which we can give emphasis for employment of our growing labour force.

In the early period of planning, eradication of exploitative elements like absentee landlordism, village money-lenders and marketing functionaries played a commendable role alongwith increased irrigation facilities to the cultivable land.

For raising agricultural productivity, co-operative farming was popularised in our country. With the green revolution, and introduction of water, seed and fertilizer technology a remarkable break-through emerged. But it has been observed that the introduction of high yielding variety of seeds and new cropping pattern, has led to some peculiar results in the employment front. The increased agricultural activities has created high demand for labour which generally becomes scarce in the peak period of sowing and harvesting (Imandar and Mulgund, Kurukshetra, July, '97). To tide over the situation of labour scarcity two important developments have taken place.

i) The well off farmers have adopted mechanization even for harvesting and processing activities. The poor farmers on the other hand, were to depend upon family labour. Thus, the small-farmers expressed their reliance on family labour.

ii) Secondly, the heavy demand of agricultural labourers led to collective bargaining of the farmers through formation of small groups. Thus, the leader of the group or the headman has to bargain with the landlord for higher wages or wages on contract basis for specified agricultural activities especially, during peak seasons of transplantation and harvesting of agricultural crops. Thus, the contractual labour system was more pronounced after the green revolution in our country. This, leads to higher wages of the agricultural labourers and also performance of works with less time. Thus, the role of headman became crucial in fixing wages for the contractual agricultural labourers. Thus, the agricultural labourers were to work in a group and expressed reluctance to work individually in the agricultural operations. However, agriculture being seasonal, there is a problem of getting continuous employment in agricultural sector by the agricultural labourers. Thus, agricultural labourers have been forced to depend on supplementary occupations mainly in the non-farm sector. They are forced to migrate to distant places in search of employment, income and livelihood. Thus, migration of agricultural labourers has become an inevitable consequence. The tribal labourers of Bolangir and Kalahandi (undivided) districts of Orissa usually migrate to Ganjam district within the state of Orissa in order to work in the brick-kiln industries and some of the tribal labourers do also migrate to Ganjam District within the state of Orissa in order to work in the brick-kiln industries and some of the tribal labourers do also migrate to Andhra Pradesh and Madhya Pradesh, the neighbouring states of Orissa (Tripathy, S.N. and Das, C.R., "Migrant Labour in India, Discovery, 1997).

Thus, the problems of pressure on land and the problem of seasonal unemployment should be tackled through the diversified agricultural activities, multiple cropping and the creation of potentialities of irrigation. Migration may not be harmful so long as it leads to better income and standard of living. But apparently, migration is considered as a detrimental factor for human development if it leads to exploitation and misery.

Studies conducted by Tripathy and Das (Migrant Labour in India, Discovery, 1997) reveal that the agricultural labourers of Orissa migrate to Surat to work in the handloom Sectors. They work overtime by putting 14 to 16 hours of labour and thereby earn more money income. But devoid to any protective laws and facilities of housing, water, sanitation they fall a victim to various types of fatal diseases and health hazards. Thus, such detrimental affects of adverse work-environment deteriorates the health, efficiency and living conditions of agricultural labourers of Ganjam district (Orissa) at last. Secondly, the tribals mainly the unskilled labourers migrate to the distant places of Andhra Pradesh, Madhya Pradesh or even to Haryana and Punjab where they are exploited by the contractors or *Khatadars* in earth works or construction projects. Thus, in human exploitation of tribal labourers were because of such rural-urban migration in search of employment and income.

Therefore, in order to arrest the trend of mass migration, employment in the non-agricultural sector should also be created.

It is mentionworthy that while there were 50,000 trade unions to fight for the cause of 28 million industrial workers with more than 150 pieces of legislation for them, more than 100 million farm labourers are devoid of any such organisation to fight for their legitimate rights and demand (Rao, Kurukshetra, July '97, p. 17).

Thus, the living conditions of agricultural labourers deteriorate except in states like Punjab and Haryana. In Punjab, shortage of agricultural labourers help to raise their wages and even in Kerala due to protective policy of the leftist Government could ameliorate the conditions of agricultural labourers. But in most of the states of India, due to rise in the price of wage funds simultaneously with the increase in the money wage, the living conditions of agricultural labourers deteriorate.

A survey by the International Labour Organisation (1977-78) reveals that 30 per cent of the agricultural labourers in India were in casual employment and their percentage has been steadily increasing. Thus, we find that due distressed living conditions and low real wages, unemployment-all these entangle the agricultural labourers in the web of misery and indebtedness.

The issue of minimum wages in a labour surplus agricultural economy of India is much relevant as about 75 per cent of India's population depend on this agricultural sector. The Minimum Wages Act has become one of the main instruments which can be applied to prevent the exploitation of labourers. It has been observed by the ILO-SAAT (1996, Chapter-2, p. 24) that wages paid to the labourers in the unorganised sector were insufficient for their existence. In India, a large proportion of poor could not lift themselves from the levels of poverty-line because of the low wages paid to them. It is, therefore, the state can play a crucial role through regulative mechanisms of Minimum Wages Act (1948) and can influence wage fixation for the unorganised labourers. However, there is absolute need to adopt the following measures for proper enforcement of the Minimum Wages Act and its various provisions (Gill and Luhumi, The Indian Journal of Labour Economics, Vol. 40, No. 4, 1997, p. 768) :

i) The Officers of the Revenue, Rural Development and other departments under the Act need to be associated with the task of enforcement in a more meaningful manner and made accountable to the labour department on this aspect of their duties. The level and extent of non-compliance as evidence by the inspection reports should be included in the annual reports on the administration of the Act.

ii) The enforcement effort should be diverted towards the low wage packets where the labour is more in need of protection rather than the areas which are more convenient to inspect.

iii) The enforcement machinery should be well co-ordinated with the Labour Inspector staff, Magistrate, Police Officer. They should be free from corruption and should be honest in their dealings so that they can restore the confidence of the poor and unorganised labourers.

iv) The prescribed rate of minimum wages should be ensured to the agricultural labourers through wide publicity and thus, awareness among the employers and labourers can created.

Finally, there is a need for periodically adjustments and enforcement of prescribed minimum wages, if the farmer is lower market wage rate or prevailing wage rate. Because most of the times the minimum wage rate is never refixed or changed according to the changes in the price level (which generally shows an increasing trend). Similarly, in the low wage pockets of inaccessible regions of Kalahandi, Bolangir and Koraput (undivided districts of Orissa), we observe that there has been distressed wage payment which is much lower the minimum wages prescribed under the Act. In such interior pockets of rural Orissa or other regions of India, the Government machinery should take strong steps for the enforcement of minimum wages in order to protect the interests of the weaker sections of the society. This is also justified in view of the social justice stand points. But the irony is that (as has been observed) the illiterate and simple tribals who are mostly unorganised, due to scarcity of wage employment and high supply of labour do accept lower wages for their existence. In such cases, the Government machinery could not able to protect their interests. In most cases, the village money lenders or the landlords have their nexus with the Police, politicians and administration and thus, ruthlessly treat the rural labourers and suppress (Tripathy, S.N., Bonded labour in India, Discovery, 1989). Therefore, the devoted non-Governmental organisations and social workers should take effective steps in creating awareness among the tribals and unorganised labourers regarding their rights, responsibilities and duties. They should right for the cause of the poverty-ridden tribals and labourers.

Because of the wide-spread poverty, assetlessness, the tribal labourers do work with the money lenders and traders, businessmen and village landlords for lower wages. Sometimes, they receive advances on standing crops with the promise to sell the agricultural crops and minor forest produces to the creditor. Thus, they could not receive remunerative price for their agricultural production. Thus, the tribal agricultural labourers who are under the contract to sell their agricultural output to specific buyers or creditors are bonded. Such exploitative bonded trade practices are common in the undivided districts of Koraput, Phulbani and Kalahandi (Orissa). The rehabilitation strategy of freed bonded labourers in Orissa has followed land-based scheme. Under the scheme some uncultivable, barren and unfertile lands are sanctioned provisionally to the freed bonded labourers for cultivation purposes. The horticulture department has been assigned the task of providing good seeds, fertilizers and other small inputs to the freed bonded labourers. But highly corrupted officials do not provide such inputs adequately and the concerned labourers with the bushy, uncultivable land develop no interest for his settlement. Such labourers relinquish the lands and migrate to other places in search or works.

Thus, the Government schemes envisaged with good intention could not be materialised because of wrong implementation strategy (Tripathy, S.N. Bonded Labour in India, Discovery, New Delhi).

Thus, it has been observed that decline in the forest area due to shifting cultivation, restrictions imposed by the Government in the use of forest, lavish expenditure for social ceremonies, disease and indebtedness are the factors which entangle the tribal agricultural labourers in the web of misery and perpetual poverty. Thus, the unorganised tribal agricultural labourers are in the midst of indebtedness and maintain a sub-human living. These observations have been made by the author during more than one decade of studies in the tribal-belts of Orissa.

In the wake of liberalisation and privatization policy adopted by the Government, it is the unorganised sector which faces the great stress and strain. Because the market forces of price regulation or price mechanism operate to induce investment in the profit-oriented, low-cost goods. The lure of profit induces to modernise the economy through the use of modern and upgraded equipments both in the farm and non-farm sectors of the economy. Thus, there is every possibility of technological upgradation leading to structural unemployment and replacement of labourers. Because under the policy of mainstreaming the Indian economy with the World economy or the policy of globalisation, cast-reduction technique are promoted and thus, in the restructuring process labourers are likely to be replaced due to capitalistic process of production. Thus, the market forces can not give justice to the labouring class in ensuring proper and rational wage. Hence, the state should play its role in order to protect the interests of the tribals and weaker sections of the society through proper wage policy.

Thus, a well co-ordinated policy of creating wage-employment on sustainable basis through water-shed management, soil-conservation, construction works etc. the state can go a long way for the well-being of the tribal labourers of Orissa and other states of India.

The cancer of corruption has eroded all moral values and eaten the vitals of the economy. Therefore, the cases of corrupted and misappropriation of Government funds should be firmly dealt with.

In the co-ordinated policy for the tribals, unorganised labourers, there should be greater percentage of expenditure for social sector like education, health, housing, old age pensions, reliefs to the victimised personal under flood, drought etc. Because such a policy can provide social justice, bring about desirable changes in the economy through reduction of inequality and protect the exploitation of the weaker sections and mostly the labouring class. Thus, through the provisions of social security safety-nets, creation of employment avenues and awareness of the tribals and unorganised agricultural labourers, we can do something meaningful for the poverty-stricken rural people.

References

1. Ghaneksar, J. (1997), "Sorry State of Agricultural Wage Data: Sources and Method of Collection", *Economic and political Weekly*, Vol. XXXII, No. 19, May 10–16.
2. Tripathy, S. N. (1997), "Minimum Wages and Agricultural Labours in Orissa", *The Indian Journal of Labour Economics* Volume 40 no. 4, Oct.–December, 97, p. 785.

Bibliography

1. Shabha, V., Rural Women and Development : A study of female agricultural labours in Telengana, Delhi, Mittal Publication, 1987.
2. Nair, N. K., Aravindakashan, Agricultural Labour in Kerala, ICSSR *Research Abstracts quarterly,* 16 (1 and 2) Jan.–June, 1987.
3. Saradamani, K., Labour, Land Rice Production : Women Involvement, *Economic and Political Weekly,* 22 (17), April 25, 1987.
4. Danekar, V.M., Kheti, Rojagari and Garibi (Agriculture, Employment and Poverty), Madhukari, 13(i), 1987.
5. Bhati, J.P. and Singh, D.V., Women's Contribution to Agricultural Economy in Hill Regions of North-West India. *Economic and Political Weekly* 22 (17), April 25, 1987.
6. Sunita & Others, Rural Women Labour : Differential Treatment by Landlord elites, *Journal of Extension Systems,* 3 (2), Dec., 1987.
7. Katre, M.M., Minimising the MInimum, *The Lawyers* 2(11), Nov., 1987.
8. George, Alex, Social and Economic Aspects of Attached Labourers in Kuttanand Agriculture, *Economic and Political Weekly,* 22(52), Dec. 26, 1987.
9. Yadav, Ramnath and Azad, M.P., Role of Women in allied enterprises for Rural Development, *Kurukshetra,* 36(2) Nov., 1987.

10. Sengupta, Devjani, Khet Majdoor Movement; A Case Study in West Bengal, *Social-Scientist* 15(7), July, 1987.
11. Singh, Harner, Agricultural workers in Punjab : Their Role and Commitment, *Indian dissertation Abstracts* 16(2), April-June, 1987.
12. Bhadra, Mita, Work, Working Facilities and Occupational Mobility among the Adivasi Women Workers of Tea Plantation. *Eastern Anthropologist* 40(2), April-June, 1987.
13. Punjabi, Jyothi and Sadhu A.N., New Agricultural Strategy and Rural Women, *Journal of Rural Development* 7(3), May, 1988.
14. Dev, S. Mehendra, Poverty of Agricultural Labours Households in India : A State Level Analysis, *Indian Journal of Agricultural Economics* 43(1), Jan.-March, 1988.
15. Politevin, Guy, Primary Health Care as a Gender Issue, *Economic and Political Weekly*, 23(44) Oct., 29, 1988.
16. Krishnamurthy, Sunanda, Wage Differentials on Agriculture by Case, Sex and Operations, *Economic and Political Weekly*, 23(50), Dec. 10, 1988.
17. Maurya, Sahab Deen, Women in India, Chug Publications, Allahabad, 1988.
18. Lalita, K. and Sharada, D., Socio-Economic and Living Conditions of Farm Labourers, *Journal of Rural Developments* 7(3), May, 1988.
19. Singh, A.K. and Others, Participation of Rural Women in Agriculture in the Hills of Uttar Pradesh, *Journal cf Rural Development*, 7(3), 1988.
20. Laxmi Devi, A., Rural Women : Management in Farm and Home, Northern Book Centre, New Delhi, 1988.
21. Gupta, A.K. and Others, Sociological Analysis of Migration of Agricultural Labourers from Eastern to North-Western Region of India, *Indian Journal of Industrial Relations*, 23(4) April, 1988.
22. Unni, Jeemol., Agricultural Labourers in Rural Labour Households 1956–57 to 1977–78 : Changes in Employment, Wages and Incomes.
23. Cherniguin, Serbe, The Sugar Workers of Negros, Phillippines, Community Development, *Journal*, 23(3), July, 1988.

24. Reddy, V. Ratna, Surplus Labour, Poverty and Agricultural Development : A Case Study of Andhra Pradesh Artha Vijana 30(4) Dec., 1988.

25. Kwon, Young-JA, A Study of Korean Rural Woman's Labour : With Special Emphasis on Farm Housewives, *Women Studies Forum*, 1988.

26. Singh, C.S.K., Building Organisation of Agricultural Labourers : Case Study of Bakhari, Mainstream, 26(37), June 25, 1988.

27. Malkit Kaur, Rural Women and Technological Advancement, Discovery Publishing House, Delhi, 1988.

28. Patil, Rajendra B., Minimum Wages for Farm Workers in Maharashtra, *Rural India*, 51(9), Sept., 1988.

29. Kalaimathi, A., Labour Force Participation of Women in Agriculture, *Journal of Ravi Sankar University*, 1(i) 1988.

30. Bhogal, T.S., and Others, Augmenting Income and Employment of Small and Marginal Farmers and Landless Agricultural Labours through Dairying in Western U.P., *The Indian Journal of Dairy Science*, 41(1) March, 1988.

31. Nair, G. Ravindran, Time Stands Still for the Women Farm Labour Social Welfare, 36(2) May, 1989.

32. Bardhan, Kalpana, Poverty, Growth and Rural Labour Markets in India : *Economic and Political Weekly*, 24(1 & 2), May 25, 1989.

33. Pandey, M.P., Problems and Prospects of Agricultural Labour in Bihar : An Analysis in the context of Minimum Wages Act. *Third Concept* 2(24), 1989.

34. Shukla, Tara, Rural Non-agricultural Employment, *Economic and Political Weekly* 24(35, 36) Sept. 2–9, 1989.

35. Sharma, Narayan Prasad, Wage Differentials for Women Agricultural Labourers, *Yojana* (33) (12), July 1–15, 1989.

36. Nikhade, Dm, and Nimje, N.R., Involvement and Consultation Farm Worker in Agriculture, *The Indian Journal of Home Science* 19(2), Dec., 1989.

37. Sharma, P. Perraju, Motivating the Poor for Education : A Study with Reference to Agricultural Labour, p. 108–117. jin Rao,

M. Kutumba and sharma P. Perraju (eds.). Human Resource Development for Rural Development Bombay, Himalaya Publications, 1989.

38. Verma, B.N., Recent Technological Change in Agricultural and Distributive Aspects, *IASSI Quarterly* 8(4), March, 1990.

39. Mowli, V. Chandra, Of Human Bondage : An Indian Experience Amongst the Agrarian Work Force. Social Action 40(2), April–June, 1990.

40. Nanchariah, G., The Changing Position of Scheduled Castes as Agricultural Labourers in the Labour Market, *Social Action* 40(2), April–June, 1990.

41. Gupta, Vishwanath, *Women Labour in Tea Plantation Social Welfare*, 37(2) June, 1990.

42. Parthasarthy, R., Labour Utilization in Tamil Nadu, *Agriculture Artha Vijmana* 32(2), June, 1990.

43. Guha, Sumit, Labour Intensity in Indian Agriculture, 1880–1970, Some Findings., *Economic and Political Weekly* 25(52), Dec., 29, 1990.

44. Ramchandran, V.K., Wage Labour in Unfreedom in Agriculture: An Indian Case Study, Clarendran Press, Oxford, 1990.

45. Kishwar, Madhu and Horowitz, Berny, Family Life of Agricultural Labourers and Small Farmers in Punjab. In Kashwar, Madhu and Vanita Rath (eds.) In Search of Answers : Indian Women's Voice from Manushi, New Delhi, Horizon India Book, 1991.

46. Chakravarty, Shubramanyu, Sanitation and Personal Hygiene: A Study of the Tribal Workers in the Tea Plantation of the Teral Region of West Bengal, *Folkore* 32(9), Sept., 1991.

47. Reddy, Sudhakar, Poverty and Agricultural Growth in Rural Andhra Pradesh (Monograph No. 1), Centre for Economic Studies, Hyderabad, (1991).

48. Reddy, M. Atchi, Work and Leisure : Daily Working Hours of Agricultural Labourers, Nellore District, 1860–1989. *The Indian Economic and Social History Review* 28(1).

49. Singh, Choudhary Charana, Kisan-Santan Ke Liye Pachas Prathishat Arakshan Kyon (Why Fifty per cent Reservation for Farmers ?) *Asli Bharat* 12(6), Month, 1991.

50. Krishan, T.N., Wages Employment and Output in Inter-related Labour Markets in An Agrarian Economy : A Study of Kerala. *Economic and Political Weekly*, 26(26), June 29, 1991.

51. Sidhy, H.S., Agricultural Development and Rural Labour : A Case Study of Punjab and Haryana, New Delhi, Concept Publication, 1991.

52. Mohanty, Nilankantha, Impact of Agro-based Industry on Farm Economy, Radha Publications, New Delhi (1995).

53. Tripathy, S.N., Pradhan, K.C., Agricultural Labour in India, Discovery Publication House, New Delhi (1996).

54. Ghanekar, J., "Sorry State of Agricultural Wage, Data : Sources and Method of Collection", *Economic and Political Weekly*, Vol. XXXII, No. 19, May 10–16 (1997).

55. Tripathy, S.N., Minimum Wages and Agricultural Labour in Orissa, *Indian Journal of Labour Econcmy*, Volume 40, No. 4, October-December, 1997.

Index